WITH 32 PLANS 5,—

Marino Marini

Universe Sculpture Series

Em. Langui   **Marino Marini**

Universe Books, Inc., New York

Horse and rider   bronze   1947   Museum of Modern Art, New York

Universe Sculpture Series is edited by Prof. A. M. Hammacher

Copyright 1959 in the Netherlands by Allert de Lange, Amsterdam
Library of Congress Catalog Card Number 59-10153
Typography and cover Otto Treumann, GKf, AGI
Printed in the Netherlands by H. Veenman & Zonen N.V., Wageningen

An encouraging phenomenon that we have seen in recent years is that sculpture, too long and too often regarded and treated as the Cinderella of the arts, has regained for itself an equal place with the art of painting. The taste of the public and the interest of the ordinary man have developed so favorably that large-scale exhibitions of sculpture in the open air (Battersea Park, London, Sonsbeek, Arnhem, Middelheim, Antwerp) now draw visitors in their thousands. This turn of affairs, which is accompanied by an unusual flowering of sculpture and of the monument in its most essential significance, enables the plastic arts to fulfil again their ancient, noble, social task. But at the same time, another consequence is that the conflict which is taking place around the problems of form has, so to speak, to be fought out in public, and the masses, whatever their prejudices and mistakes, have become actively involved in the struggle for a new style, a struggle which chiefly turns on the question: representational or abstract?

Now the verdicts of two international juries of important public artistic events have recently caused us surprises. In 1951 the world prize for sculpture was awarded by the 'Primiera Bienal de Arte Moderna' at Sâo Paulo to the Swiss Brazilian architect and sculptor Max Bill for his 'Threefold Trinity', a typical non-representational creation; a double spiral in stainless metal, turning in space like a falling silver flame. With this event, for the first time in this century, the seal was set more or less officially on the triumph of abstract sculpture.

This verdict was confirmed a year later by another equally international jury, when the American, Alexander Calder, with his well-known metal 'Mobiles' and 'Stabiles', won the big prize at the *XXVIe* Biennale at Venice, over the heads of Lipchitz, Germaine Richier, Wotruba, Probst and other more or less representational sculptors. But at the same time the jury expressed its regret that the rules exclude all Italians from the 'Grande premio' and expressed the hope of seeing this indefensible clause (that seems to date from the time of Mussolini) withdrawn. What or who had given rise to this attitude adopted by experts from more than twenty countries of Europe and overseas? Who was the Italian whose work had occasioned this incident and who had to be contented with the prize of the city of Venice? Both prizes have the same value – one million lire; but on an international level they have naturally not the same renown. It detracts in no way from the very special significance of Calder's work, when we assert that in actual fact the moral winner at Venice was Marino Marini. Here we are faced again with the problem of representational as against non-representational art. Naturally the first task of an international jury is to judge the artists according to their individual merits, yet its verdicts in many respects set the standard for the general tendency of the age, and this seems, above all, to follow what Taine describes as 'the work of art that is sufficiently true to reality to recall to us the natural image and at the same time far enough from reality to make us dream'. Can a better description of the work of Marino Marini be conceived?

Scarcely ten years ago he was little known or quite unknown outside Italy, and even in Italy he was known only to small circles in Milan, Rome and Venice. It is true that during the last war his fame penetrated to Switzerland and that the Basel Art Gallery bought his 'Archangel' in 1943: but this is partly due to the fact that the artist, after his studio had been destroyed twice in air attacks, had fled to Switzerland.

These painful wartime experiences, and an airplane accident near the coast of Greece, seem to be the only adventures in the artist's life who, although he travels a great deal (France, Belgium, The Netherlands, England, Switzerland, Germany, Austria, Sweden, Greece and the United States) has once and for all devoted all the intensity of his life to his art. Born at Pistoja in Tuscany on February 27th, 1901, he is already more than fifty, yet one would easily take him for at least ten years younger, so youthful, so fresh and energetic and so sportive is his whole appearance glowing with health and the lust for life. His open face, his honest expression, his ringing laugh at once win everybody's liking. Moreover he is simplicity personified, to the point of shyness, and yet amazingly sure of himself where his work is concerned.

This work he had first and foremost to learn as a difficult skill, for although Alain maybe right when he says that sculpture is the artistic form in which amazing results can be most quickly and easily achieved, yet it is an arduous and intricate craft, in which manual dexterity, strength of wrist, precision of movement and sharpness of eye, play as great a role as does what is generally known as inspiration. More than is the case with other artists, must the sculptor's muscles be completely under the control of his spirit. A sculptor's career is always quite different from a painter's: Marini's also. At the same time they remain closer to the medieval idea of a master-craftsman than their confreres who wield the palette.

Marini began his studies at the Academie Belle Arti in Florence, where he both painted and carved. But whether he received much more than a thorough technical training from his teachers is doubtful, although it is not impossible that they opened his eyes to the weak, over-sensitive style of Medardo Rosso, who though he had passed the zenith of his career, nevertheless continued to exercise a certain attraction for the younger generation. Marino Marini, in the beginning at least, also fell under the charm of the pictorial impressionism of this artist who stated that 'nothing is material in space. Everything is pure life and air. Nothing is outlined. Everything is movement'. This influence affected Marini firstly as painter and draftsman, as for many years he was, above all, to draw, paint and etch. He was already turning thirty, when sculpture began to take first place with him, a fact of the greatest importance in the development of his style.

If one wishes to judge Marini's plastic art at its full worth, one must never lose sight of the fact that he is always sculptor and painter at one and the same time; that is to say that his feelings – the source of all art – arise equally from color as from form, and that throughout his life he seeks in his work to unite both elements in an inevitable harmony. The word harmony is perhaps not well chosen, for in all polychrome sculpture, be it Greek Roman, Eastern or Baroque, color and form harmonize. But for Marini the aim is different. He does not seek a compromise between the colors of reality and the painted image, but uses color more and more as an independent element which becomes the counterpoint of form in the design.

Expressed more simply, the colors do not meekly cover the forms, they cut across the image in an independent rhythm, full of life and imagination. How Marini manages to keep both these elements in complete harmony is one of the mysteries of his art.

For the most part indeed the creation of color element precedes that of the plastic element. With few exceptions he first interprets his emotions in a long series of sketches, pen-drawings, gouaches, and oil-paintings all turning on the same theme. In endless variations of color and design he approaches the statue-to-be from all points of view until it has matured in his mind, that is until it has acquired a third dimension. Then only comes the stage of chipping or modelling, yet even as he works the statue grows independently, obedient to purely plastic laws of form and light, of tension and repose, of attack on – and retreat from – space. And when the form is finished, in plaster, wood or bronze (Marino rarely uses stone) then begins the subtle working of the surface, the chiseling, the patinating and the coloring. For this artist a statue is, in fact, never finished. Not only does he repeatedly make changes on the surface of works from earlier years, such as the Ersilia, begun in 1931 and finished in 1949: but also he is unable to see one of his works in a collection without the desire coming upon him to seize his chisel and for the sheer joy in the continuous act of creation, to do one or another plane over again.

This long digression into the pictorial aspect of most of Marini's work, even where no spot of color is to be found, serves to underline with emphasis what others before us have already said, namely, that this sculptor is at the same time one of the most remarkable painters of our times. His nervous etchings and pen-drawings, his vivid gouaches and impressive canvasses, devoted to the same themes which inspire his statues, certainly belong to the most striking creations of post-expressionism in Europe.

His flaming palette, in which at one moment wine red, purple, orange and broken white are paramount, and at another indigo, grey and brown are the dominant colors, testifies to the exuberant, instinctive painter's temperament, which with the exception perhaps of Sironi, but then in a minor key, has not its equal in Italian art of today.

Many admirers of Marino Marini rank him higher as painter than as sculptor, which does not mean that his work, especially in the plastic art, is not of enormous revolutionary significance.

In all honesty we must admit that there are some who deny the revolutionary character of his sculpture. Purists, always able to find a fault somewhere, point scornfully to the different influences which Marini has undoubtedly undergone, the colored terracotta figures of the Etruscans, the ancient portrait busts of the empire, the plastic works of the Weis and the T'angs and the naturalistic masks of the fourteenth century. Why not include the whole British Museum? For our part we can also add that Marini is an enthusiastic admirer of Pre-Columbian art. But what does all this signify? Is the work of a great artist who also happens to be heir to one of the most splendid of Western cultures, less good, less pure, because his inspiration corresponds to that of some of the creations of the past? Why should his art be called reactionary, as opposed to the art which, delving into pre-history, is inspired by totem poles, Negro sculpture and the elementary forms of the mineral world? Are we no longer able to regard a work of art as a plastic fact in and for itself, instead of as a more-or-less suitable phase in an evolution whose end no-one can foresee? For instance, after Brancusi cannot all representational art be called in a certain sense reactionary? But let us leave this fruitless discussion – in the first place it leaves Marini quite cold – and let us try to explain the immense significance of his sculpture as a very personal independent phenomenon and very important one.

Marino Marini's earliest important terracotta statues such as the group Popolo (1929), a married couple standing, already betray, in spite of the classical Roman composition and pose and the characteristic air of the persons represented, an inner tension and a fierce urge for self-expression, which so clearly distinguishes them from Arturo Martini's soft over-sensitive sculpture of the same period. At the same time they have a popular, strongly naturalistic character which is not far removed from the expressionism of the Ersilia (1931). This powerful dignified statue of a woman, with its full, heavy form, was the starting point of a long series of portrait busts unique in the art of today.

The human countenance, considered as the purest individual mirror of the soul, of character, of an attitude to life, has in fact found no master since the death of Rodin, to produce anything worthy of the head of Balzac, of Clemenceau, or of Rochefort. But in Marini we find one who, while he works continually at the perfecting of a synthetic style, divorced from realistic and anecdotal accidents, is yet repeatedly intrigued by the amazing, unique and exciting phenomenon of the human mask, that inexhaustible source of sculptural and psychological possibilities. It is as though Marini were obsessed by portrait-making, which he practices with a virtuosity, a cunning and a love which have inspired his finest, most striking creations. They are acts of faith, of friendship and admiration for those whom he loves: his distinguished cultivated wife Marina: his comrades, painters and sculptors, the old futurist Carrà, the dreamy de Pisis, Campigli with his athlete's head, the sculptor Melotti, the fine landscape painter Tosi, the Milan art dealer Cardazzo, Madame Hahnloser who has gathered together one of the finest collections in Europe, Georg Schmidt the friendly director of the Museum at Basel, Igor Stravinsky and many others, figures of young girls, of men and women of the intelligentsia. Each one of these portraits is not only a typical document; but each in its turn is executed in a completely new style as though unconsciously the model has imposed the technique on the artist. The style is a subtle mixture of impressionism, archaism and modernism, which makes of them something timeless, intensely alive and unforgettable, which though illustrative of our epoch is yet difficult to place in the evolution of this century. From every point of view Marini is an exception.

His numerous, robust studies of the nude, his Pomonas and Venuses, his dancers, and acrobats, his girls bathing which, even more than his portraits, have established his fame, are created in the same mysterious style; a style difficult to define, since we find in him to a certain degree a synthesis of many currents and tendencies. This does not mean that Marini's style is the result of a selection from old and dead cultures, as is, for instance, that of Bourdelle.

On the contrary, Marini's enormous power of persuasion lies precisely in the aliveness of his works, in the warm, healthy, radiant sensuality which animates the inert matter. This latent life does not only vibrate on the surface; it fills the whole volume, supports the figure, spans the forms from within outwards and gives to the unmoving, ponderous image something of the calm elemental power of nature, with all its wildness curbed yet filled to overflowing with the robust energy of life.

Not for nothing are most of his standing nudes called Pomona, for no other title could symbolize these over-ripe, healthily sensual, supremely maternal female figures. They bear in them the ancient, blind mystery which palaeolithic man already tried to interpret in the Venus of Willendorf. That is the secret of the spiritual quality of Marini's art; in it he pays homage to the highest biological law of creation, virile, honest and simple.

Affectation is foreign to his nature and he never hesitates, where it is fitting, to exaggerate the deformities of life without which, according to Baudelaire, 'il n'y a pas de beauté', and now and then, as if Pan should go into a retreat, he creates purely spiritualized figures, full of a Gothic mysticism, ecstasy and pain, such as the Miracle and both Archangels, in which are found the sober dramatic quality of the old Roman sculpture. Such statues silence and disarm those who seek to reproach Marini's art with its so-called materialism.

Besides the portraits, the nudes, the conjurers and the dancers, his horses and riders form a group apart, extremely powerful. In this field he is without doubt at his most individual, and with these works above all he has drawn upon himself the keenest interest of the whole art world. With a furious creative energy he has been working, since 1936, at an impressive hymn to the horse. More and more he seems to want to devote his life's task to the noblest conquest of man and he is enthusiastic about the art of, for instance, the T'ang period when the horse stood as high in a sculptor's eyes as did the dancers of the Imperial corps de ballet. No other theme has stimulated Marini so strongly, both plastically and emotionally and nowhere else has his style followed a more complicated evolution. At first purely frontal and static, as in archaic Roman sculpture, form and pose incline more and more to the early Chinese burial ceramics of the Han period, soberly stylized, monumental and full of movement. He makes increasing use of deformation and exaggeration; man and beast seem to grow together till they become one whole, always more dynamic, more nervous, to be caught up at last in a wild baroque expressionism of pure rhythm and power. Every one of these centaur figures is like a living pyramid in which lines, planes and forms strive towards one single point in which is concentrated the whole wild ecstasy.

Horse and rider seem to be taking part in an ancient ceremony of sun worship, so tensely and passionately does the whole image reach out towards the heights. Everyone must see how each of these riders, with upturned face, tries to embrace infinity with a longing passionate gesture. There lies, I don't know what of primitive and deeply human ardor in these statues, something that goes back into the night of time, something of the joyous faith of earliest man when he sprang to horse in a race to meet the eternal dawn.

Many hundreds of drawings, gouaches and oil studies precede the sculpture, and especially in recent years the statues in their turn are covered with a bright irrational polychrome like a shrill cry of triumph. Marini comes here very close to Picasso, who before and after Guernica, devoted some of his most moving and dramatic canvasses, etchings and drawings to the horse. But for the Spanish master the inspiration lies in the tragic aspect of the beast, martyred in the arena or during the revolution, reaching out to the sun in a last wild convulsion.

With Marini, on the other hand, all his statues of riders are focused upon life, positive, passionate and overwhelming in their self-confidence. And yet, in spite of this basic difference between their two temperaments – that also implies a difference in their attitudes of life – both styles are much more closely related than appears at first sight. Both artists are followers of a baroque expressionism, which, with abstract art, seems to be the only language in which the art of the tragic heroic period in which we live can express itself.

It would of course be a mistake to attribute other than purely plastic aims to Marino Marini. He is as far from the 'artistes engagés' as from the ivory towers of the abstractionist. Whoever loves life as honestly and simply as he does, discovers unintentionally some of the great truths of the time in which he believes, even though his intention is to concentrate all his effort exclusively on the problems of form. Generations to come will certainly find this epoch most clearly reflected in the work of those who have practised art for art's sake without any secondary motives or digressions; Brancusi, Picasso, Laurens, Lipchitz, Moore, Zadkine, Calder, Richier, Marino Marini and half a dozen other figures, to confine ourselves to sculptors only.

There is no point in trying to decide who amongst them is more and who less great; one thing in my opinion is certain: the story of modern sculpture can no longer be written without a very important place being given to the impressive art of Marino Marini, the fifty-year-young man, who is now entering his second youth, bravely, courageously working at a glorious life task full of an enthusiasm of which his twin sister speaks in the following lines: 'In Questo spasimo forse potranno – almeno – rovinare sul mondo e diventarvi eroi.' *

Em. Langui

* In this convulsion we can pour ourselves out over the whole world and become heroes.

Illustrations

I **Ersilia** bois polychromé   1931-1949
polychrome wood
polychromiertes Holz
gepolychromeerd hout

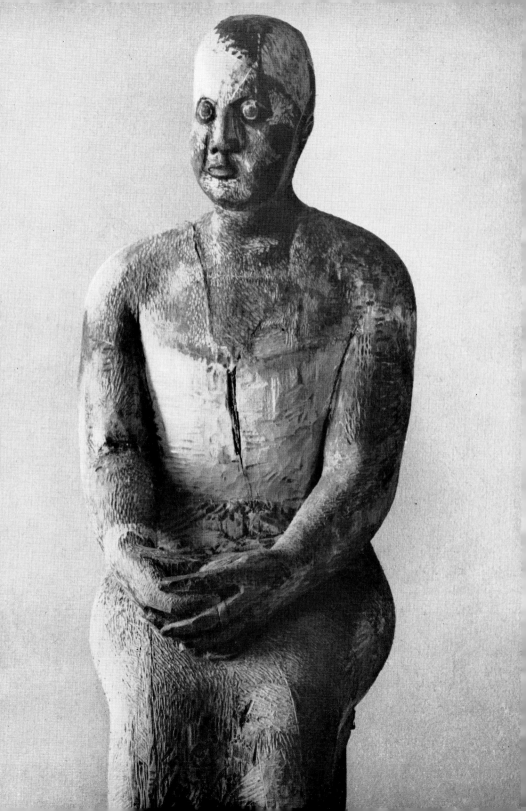

2 **Cavalier**   bois polychromé   1936   coll. Emilio Jesi, Milano
  Horseman polychrome wood
  Reiter   polychromiertes Holz
  Ruiter   gepolychromeerd hout

3 **Gentilhomme à cheval**   bronze   1937   Museum, Stockholm
  Nobleman on horseback
  Edelmann zu Pferde
  Edelman te paard

4 **Pomona**   bronze   1940   coll. Emilio Jesi, Milano

5 **Pomona** bronze 1940 Koninklijke Musea voor Schone Kunsten, Brussel

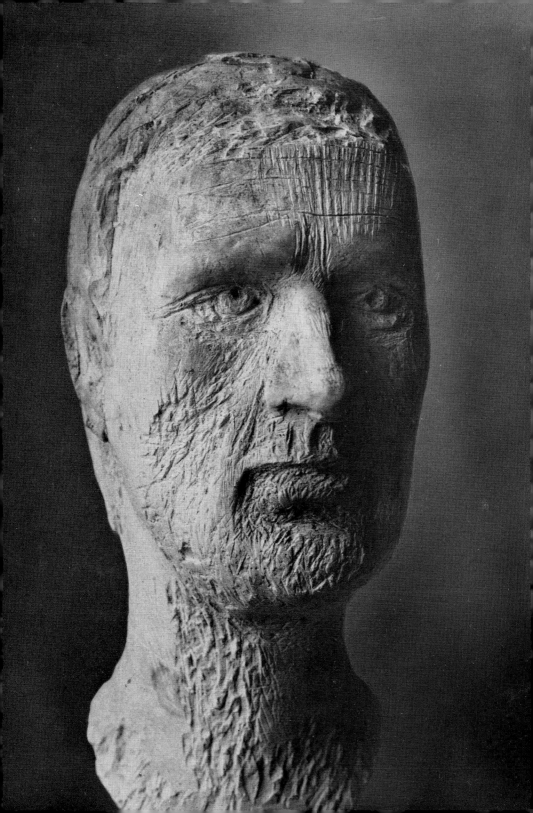

7 **l'Archange** plâtre 1943 Kunstmuseum, Basel
  Archangel plaster
  Erzengel Gips
  Aartsengel gips

8 **Archangel**   plâtre   1943
plaster
Gips
gips

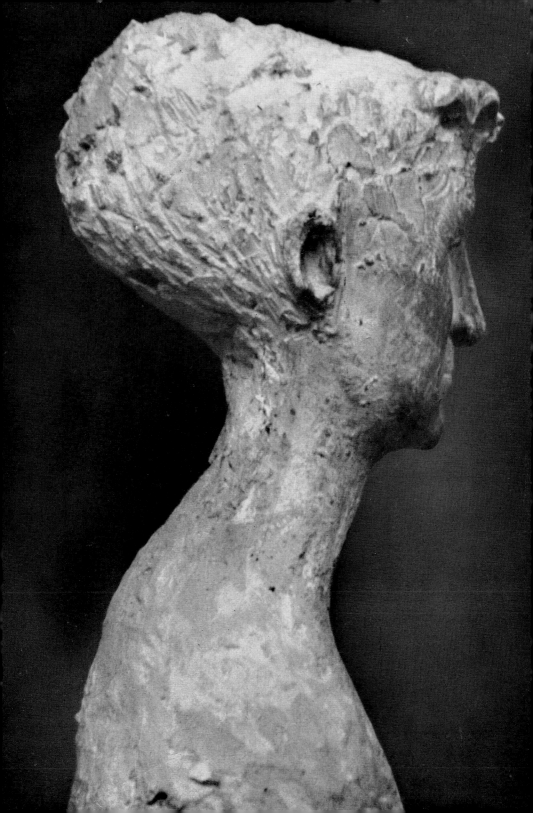

9 **Le miracle**   plâtre   1943   coll. Emilio Jesi, Milano
  The miracle   plaster
  Das Wunder   Gips
  Het wonder   gips

10 **Susanna** plâtre 1943 Curt Valentin Gallery, New York
plaster
Gips
gips

11 **Le jongleur** bronze polychromé 1944 coll. Mrs Grace, Philadelphia
 The juggler

12 **Dame** plâtre polychromé 1945
Lady polychrome plaster
polychromierter Gips
gepolychromeerd gips

13 **Nu assis** bronze 1945 Koninklijk Museum voor schone kunsten,
Sitting nude Antwerpen
Sitzende Nackte
Zittend naakt

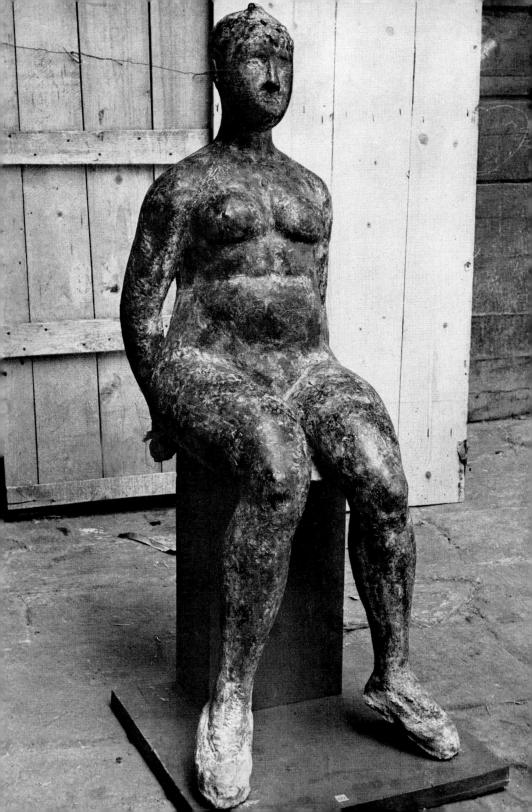

14 **Madame Jeker** plomb 1947 coll. Jeker, Milano
lead
Blei
lood

15 **Cavalier**   bronze 1947 | coll. John D. Rockefeller, New York
   Horseman | The Tate Gallery, London
   Reiter | Henry Hope, Bloomington, Indiana U.S.A.
   Ruiter |

16 **Cavalier** bronze 1947 coll. Riccardo Juker, Milano
Horseman
Reiter
Ruiter

17 **Pomona** plâtre 1948-49 Propriété de l'artiste
plaster Property of the artist
Gips Im Besitz des Künstlers
gips eigendom van de kunstenaar

18 **Danseuse** bronze 1949 coll. J. T. Soby, Farmington, Conn. U.S.A.
   Dancer   Curt Valentin Gallery, New York
   Tänzerin
   Danseres

19 **Cavalier** bronze 1949-50 coll. Sturcis Ingersoll, Philadelphia
Horseman Curt Valentin Gallery, New York
Reiter
Ruiter

20	**Cavalier**	bois polychromé	1949-50
	Horseman	polychrome wood	
	Reiter	polychromiertes Holz	
	Ruiter	gepolychromeerd hout	

21 **Tête** bronze 1950
   Head
   Kopf
   Kop

22 **Cheval** bronze 1950
   Horse
   Pferd
   Paard

23 **Igor Stravinski**   bronze   1950   San Francisco Museum of Art

24 **Cavalier**   bronze   1951   Hannover Gallery London
   Horseman   variante: Curt Valentin Gallery, New York
   Reiter
   Ruiter

25 **Jongleuse**   bronze   1951   Curt Valentin Gallery, New York
Juggler

26 **Cavalier en forme de triangle** 1951 plâtre polychromé Propriété de l'artiste,
   Horseman in the form of a triangle   bronze, coll. Baronesse Lambert,
   Reiter in Form einer Triangel   Estorick-London,   [Bruxelles,
   Ruiter in driehoeksvorm   Curt Valentin Gallery, New York

27 **Grand cheval**   bronze 1951   coll. Nelson A. Rockefeller, Tarrytown, N.Y.
   Large horse   Francisco Matarazzo Sobrinko, Sâo Paulo
   Grosses Pferd
   Groot paard

28 **Danceuze** bronze 1953
Dancer
Tänzerin
Danseres

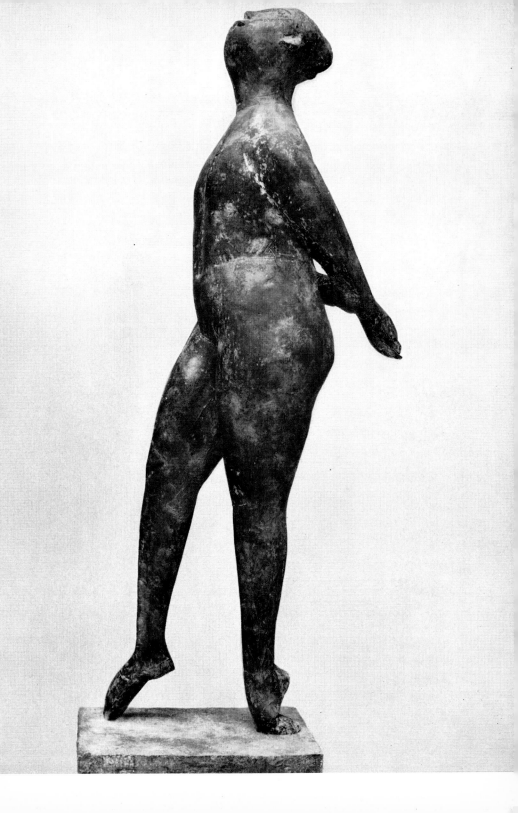

30 **Femme, cheval et cavalier** peinture à l'huile et tempera 1950
Woman, horse and rider painting in oils and tempera
Frau, Pferd und Reiter Gemälde in Öl und Tempera
Vrouw, paard en ruiter olieverf en tempera

32 **Cheval** peinture à l'huile   1952
   Horse painting in oils
   Pferd Ölgemälde
   Paard olieverf